TRAVEL PUGLIA

PUGLIA

40+ Cool Things To See And Do In
Puglia

Ted Paul

TABLE OF CONTENT

Introduction

  Why Puglia is Worth Visiting

Chapter 1: Food and Drink

  Eat Fresh Seafood in Bari

  Visit a Local Winery in Salento

  Try Pasticciotto in Lecce

  Discover the Flavor of Taralli

Chapter 2: Beaches and Coastline

  Explore the White City of Ostuni

  Take a Dip in the Crystal-Clear Waters of Polignano a Mare

  Relax on the Sandy Shores of Torre Lapillo

  Admire the Natural Beauty of Gargano National Park

Chapter 3: History and Culture

  Wander the Streets of Alberobello's Trulli

  Visit the Historic Castle of Otranto

  Marvel at the Baroque Architecture of Lecce

  Explore the Roman Ruins of Egnazia

Chapter 4: Outdoor Activities

  Hike the Ravines of Matera

  Bike Along the Apulian Aqueduct Cycle Path

  Go Scuba Diving in Santa Maria di Leuca

  Experience the Thrill of Kitesurfing in Otranto

Chapter 5: Festivals and Events

  Celebrate the Feast of St. Nicholas in Bari

  Attend the Taranta Music Festival in Salento

Experience the Carnival of Putignano

Watch the Festa di San Pardo Horse Race in Galatina

Chapter 6: Shopping and Markets

Browse the Local Produce at Bari's Mercato Coperto

Shop for Handmade Pottery in Grottaglie

Visit the Weekly Market in Ostuni

Find Unique Souvenirs in Monopoli's Historic Center

Chapter 7: Hidden Gems

Explore the Abandoned Village of Craco

Discover the Underground Caves of Castellana Grotte

Relax at the Thermal Baths of Santa Cesarea Terme

Visit the Coastal Village of Polignano a Mare

Conclusion: Planning Your Puglia Adventure

Best Time to Visit Puglia
Puglia's Climate:
Peak Season vs. Off-Season:
Recommended Months for Specific Activities:

Getting to and Around Puglia
Airports in Puglia:
Trains and Buses in Puglia:
Driving in Puglia:
Bicycle Rentals and Tours:

Where to Stay in Puglia
Types of Accommodation:
Recommended Areas to Stay in Puglia:
Unique Accommodation Options:

Tips for Traveling in Puglia.

Introduction

Welcome to Puglia, one of Italy's hidden gems and a region that is not to be missed. Situated in the southeast of the country, Puglia boasts some of the most breathtaking scenery, delicious food and wine, and fascinating history and culture. From stunning beaches and coastline to ancient ruins and charming towns, there are so many cool things to see and do in Puglia.

This book, "40+ Cool Things to See and Do in Puglia", is your guide to exploring the region's best attractions and experiences. Whether you're a foodie, history buff, outdoor enthusiast, or just looking for a unique travel experience, there's something in Puglia for everyone.

The food and drink alone make Puglia worth a visit. From fresh seafood in Bari to local wineries in Salento and the unique flavor of Taralli, you'll experience the authentic taste of Italy. And with a coastline stretching for hundreds of kilometers, you can explore the sandy shores of Torre Lapillo or take a dip in the crystal-clear waters of Polignano a Mare.

Puglia is also a region steeped in history and culture, with ancient architecture, ruins, and towns that are simply breathtaking. Discover the trulli of Alberobello, the baroque architecture of Lecce, and the Roman ruins of Egnazia.

For outdoor enthusiasts, Puglia offers plenty of adventure, from hiking the ravines of Matera to kitesurfing in Otranto. And for those looking for a unique cultural experience, Puglia hosts a number of festivals and events throughout the year, such as the Taranta Music Festival and the Festa di San Pardo Horse Race.

This book will not only help you plan your Puglia adventure, but also provide insider tips and recommendations to help you get the most out of your trip. So, come explore the hidden treasures of Puglia and experience the authentic charm and beauty of southern Italy.

Why Puglia is Worth Visiting

Puglia, the southern region of Italy, is one of the most beautiful and culturally rich areas of the country. The region has been home to many civilizations throughout history, including the Greeks, Romans, and Byzantines, who have left a profound impact on the area's art, architecture, and culture.

One of the main attractions of Puglia is its stunning coastline, which stretches for over 800 km and features some of the most beautiful beaches in the country. The Adriatic Sea on the east and the Ionian Sea on the south offer a plethora of opportunities for beach lovers, water sports enthusiasts, and sun worshippers. Whether you prefer rocky coves, sandy shores, or rugged cliffs, Puglia's coastline has something for everyone.

Aside from its beaches, Puglia is also famous for its historical and architectural heritage. The region boasts some of Italy's finest examples of Romanesque, Gothic, and Baroque architecture, with many impressive churches, palaces, and castles dotting the landscape. One of the most unique features of Puglia's architecture is the traditional trulli houses, which are made of dry stone and have distinctive conical roofs. These charming structures have become an icon of the region and have been designated a UNESCO World Heritage Site.

The food in Puglia is also a highlight of the region. The cuisine is characterized by fresh, locally sourced ingredients, and a focus on seafood due to the region's proximity to the sea. Dishes such as orecchiette pasta with broccoli rabe, seafood risotto, and octopus stew are all must-tries. Puglia is also home to a range of delicious pastries and desserts, including the famous pasticciotto from Lecce.

In this book, we'll take you on a journey through 42 cool things to see and do in Puglia, including exploring the charming towns of Ostuni and Martina Franca, discovering the natural beauty of the Gargano Peninsula, and visiting the mysterious Castel del Monte. We'll also introduce you to some of the region's best beaches, restaurants, and cultural attractions, so you can experience the best that Puglia has to offer. So pack your bags and get ready for an unforgettable adventure in one of Italy's most underrated regions.

Chapter 1: Food and Drink

When it comes to food and drink, Puglia is a true paradise for travelers. From fresh seafood to delicious pastries, this region has something to offer for every foodie out there. Here are some must-try culinary experiences in Puglia:

Eat Fresh Seafood in Bari

Bari is a vibrant city located on the Adriatic Sea and is one of the most important cultural and economic hubs of Puglia. One of the main reasons to visit this city is to experience its culinary culture, especially its seafood. Bari has a long-standing history of fishing and seafood is an integral part of the city's culinary tradition.

One of the best things to do in Bari is to head to the port and visit the seafood markets. The markets are filled with stalls selling fresh fish, squid, mussels, and a variety of other seafood. You can witness the fishermen unloading their daily catch and witness the hustle and bustle of the market.

Once you have explored the market, it's time to head to one of Bari's many seafood restaurants to sample some of the best seafood dishes in the region. There are numerous seafood restaurants throughout the city, ranging from small family-run establishments to more upscale restaurants.

Some of the must-try dishes include the classic seafood risotto, which is made with locally sourced rice and fresh seafood. Another popular dish is the "calamarata", a pasta dish made with squid and tomato sauce. Other dishes include the "orecchiette alle cozze", a pasta dish made with mussels and the "frittura mista", a mixed seafood platter which includes fried fish, squid, and shrimp.

One of the most unique seafood dishes in Bari is the raw sea urchin. This delicacy is served in a special way, the urchin is opened and the raw flesh is eaten directly from the shell with a spoon. The sea urchin has a delicate and sweet taste that pairs well with a glass of chilled white wine.

In addition to its seafood dishes, Bari is also famous for its homemade pasta. The local pasta, called orecchiette, is made by hand and is shaped like small ears. It is usually served with a tomato-based sauce or with fresh seafood.

Apart from the traditional seafood dishes, Bari is also famous for its street food. The city has many small street vendors selling a variety of delicious snacks and light meals. One of the most popular street foods is "panzerotti", a small deep-fried calzone filled with tomato sauce and mozzarella cheese. Another popular street food is "focaccia barese", a thick flatbread topped with tomatoes, olives, and onions.

If you're looking for a unique dining experience, head to one of Bari's many seafood festivals. These festivals are held throughout the year and offer a chance to sample a variety of seafood dishes from the region. The most famous festival is the "Festa di San Nicola", which is held in May and features a variety of seafood dishes and other local specialties.

In addition to the seafood, Bari is also known for its wine. The region produces some excellent wines, including the Primitivo and Negroamaro varieties. Many restaurants in Bari offer a selection of local wines to pair with your meal.

Visit a Local Winery in Salento

If you're a wine enthusiast, a visit to a local winery in Salento is a must-do activity while in Puglia. Salento is home to some of the best wineries in Italy, producing a variety of wines from red to white, rose, and sparkling wines. However, the most famous and highly regarded wine in the region is Primitivo, a rich and fruity red wine.

Visiting a winery in Salento gives you the opportunity to learn about the winemaking process, from grape to bottle. Many wineries offer guided tours of their vineyards, where you can learn about the different grape varieties grown in the region and the techniques used to cultivate them. You can also visit the cellars where the wine is aged and stored, and learn about the different barrels and methods used in the winemaking process.

After the tour, it's time to sample some of the region's finest wines. Wineries often have a tasting room where you can sample different wines and learn about their characteristics and flavors. The knowledgeable staff will guide you through the tasting, explaining the different notes and aromas in each wine and providing recommendations for food pairings.

Visiting a winery in Salento is not only a great way to learn about wine but also to immerse yourself in the local culture. Many wineries are family-owned and operated, and you'll have the opportunity to meet the owners and hear their stories. You'll also have the chance to see the beautiful countryside of Salento and enjoy the stunning views of the vineyards and rolling hills.

There are many wineries to choose from in Salento, each offering a unique experience. Some wineries offer traditional tours and tastings, while others provide more immersive experiences like grape stomping, cooking classes, or vineyard walks.

One of the most popular wineries to visit in Salento is the Candido Winery, located in the heart of the Salento region.

Candido Winery has been producing wine for over 90 years, and its vineyards span over 170 hectares. The winery offers guided tours of its cellars, vineyards, and tasting room, where you can sample its famous Primitivo and other wines.

Another great winery to visit is the Leone de Castris Winery, the oldest winery in Puglia. Founded in 1665, Leone de Castris is steeped in history and tradition. The winery offers guided tours of its historic cellars and vineyards, as well as tastings of its award-winning wines.

If you're looking for a more immersive experience, Masseria Amastuola is a winery and farm that offers vineyard walks, cooking classes, and wine tastings. The winery is located in the countryside near the town of Crispiano and produces a variety of wines, including Primitivo, Negroamaro, and Fiano.

Whether you're a seasoned wine connoisseur or a beginner, a visit to a local winery in Salento is a great way to experience the flavors and culture of Puglia. You'll learn about the history and techniques of winemaking in the region, sample some of the finest wines, and enjoy the beautiful scenery and hospitality of the local wineries.

Try Pasticciotto in Lecce

Pasticciotto is a must-try dessert for anyone visiting the region of Puglia, especially the city of Lecce. This sweet pastry is an icon of the local cuisine, and many bakers and patisseries have been making it for generations.

The pastry shell of the Pasticciotto is made with flour, sugar, and butter, which are combined to form a soft and crumbly texture. The filling is made with custard cream, which is a mixture of eggs, sugar, and milk that is cooked until it thickens. The custard is then flavored with lemon or vanilla extract, giving it a delicate and fragrant taste.

Pasticciotto can be found in many bakeries and cafes around Lecce, but it's important to try it from a trusted and traditional pastry shop to fully appreciate the flavor and texture. One of the most famous pastry shops in Lecce is Pasticceria Natale, which has been making Pasticciotto since 1890.

Pasticciotto is typically enjoyed as a breakfast pastry or as an afternoon snack. It pairs perfectly with a cup of espresso or a glass of sweet wine, such as a Primitivo or a Moscato.

If you're feeling adventurous, try making Pasticciotto at home with a traditional recipe. Many bakeries in Lecce sell pre-made Pasticciotto shells, so all you need to do is make the custard cream filling and bake it. This is a great way to bring a piece of Puglia home with you and impress your friends and family with your culinary skills.

In addition to the traditional custard filling, some pastry shops in Lecce also offer Pasticciotto with different flavors, such as chocolate, almond paste, and Nutella. These variations offer a modern twist on the classic dessert while still maintaining its traditional shape and texture.

Pasticciotto is not only a delicious dessert, but it also has cultural significance in the region. It is considered a symbol of the city of Lecce and its culinary heritage. In fact, every year in August, Lecce hosts a festival called Festa del Pasticciotto, where locals and tourists alike can sample different variations of the dessert from various bakeries and patisseries.

Discover the Flavor of Taralli

Taralli is a staple food of Puglia, Italy and is considered as one of the most popular snacks in the region. This savory biscuit is a must-try for anyone visiting Puglia. Taralli is typically made with flour, olive oil, white wine, and flavored with various herbs and spices, such as fennel, black pepper, and chili flakes.

The shape of the taralli is circular and the dough is usually twisted or formed into a ring shape before being baked to perfection. The texture of the taralli is hard and crunchy, making it an ideal snack to munch on anytime during the day.

There are many different varieties of taralli available in Puglia, each with its unique flavor and texture. The most common varieties include taralli al finocchio (fennel-flavored taralli), taralli al peperoncino (chili-flavored taralli), and taralli al nero di seppia (taralli flavored with squid ink).

Taralli is easily available in local markets and bakeries across Puglia. It is often served as an appetizer in restaurants or cafes, and pairs perfectly with a glass of wine or a cold beer.

Moreover, Taralli makes for a perfect souvenir to take back home from Puglia. You can find them in beautiful packaging that makes them an ideal gift for friends and family.

Apart from being a delicious snack, taralli also has a cultural significance in Puglia. It is a traditional food that has been enjoyed by locals for generations. In fact, taralli-making is considered an art in Puglia, and many families have their own recipes that have been passed down through generations.

In addition to being a snack, taralli is also used in various traditional dishes in Puglia. For example, it is often crushed and used as a topping for salads or pasta dishes. Taralli crumbs are also used as a coating for fried dishes, such as meatballs or chicken cutlets.

If you are interested in learning more about taralli and its cultural significance in Puglia, you can visit one of the many workshops or factories that produce taralli. These workshops offer a unique experience where you can see how taralli is made from scratch, and even try making it yourself.

Taralli is a unique and delicious snack that is a must-try when visiting Puglia. Its savory and crunchy texture, combined with its rich flavors, make it a perfect snack to enjoy on its own or paired with a drink. Whether you are a foodie or simply looking for a tasty and authentic Italian snack, taralli is definitely worth a try.

Whether you're a foodie or just someone who appreciates good cuisine, Puglia is the perfect destination for you. With a rich culinary tradition and a variety of flavors to discover, there's no shortage of food and drink experiences to enjoy in this beautiful region.

Chapter 2: Beaches and Coastline

Explore the White City of Ostuni

Ostuni, also known as the "White City" for its whitewashed buildings, is a beautiful town situated on a hilltop overlooking the Adriatic Sea. The town's historic center, with its narrow winding streets, white buildings, and charming little squares, is a joy to explore on foot.

One of the most stunning sights in Ostuni is the Cathedral of Santa Maria Assunta, located at the highest point of the town. The cathedral features a beautiful rose window and a Baroque-style façade, and inside, you can see several important artworks and relics.

Another highlight of Ostuni is its numerous terraces and viewpoints, which offer stunning panoramic views of the surrounding countryside and coastline. One of the best places to enjoy these views is at the town's panoramic terrace, located near the cathedral.

Ostuni also has a vibrant cultural scene, with several museums, galleries, and art exhibitions throughout the year. One of the most interesting is the Museum of Preclassical Civilizations of Southern Murgia, which showcases the region's ancient history and archaeological findings.

Additionally, Ostuni is known for its excellent cuisine, with many restaurants serving traditional Puglian dishes made with local ingredients. Don't miss out on trying some of the town's specialties, such as orecchiette pasta with turnip greens, or the local seafood dishes.

Exploring the White City of Ostuni is a must-do activity in Puglia. With its picturesque streets, stunning views, and rich cultural heritage, Ostuni is a town that will leave you with unforgettable memories

Take a Dip in the Crystal-Clear Waters of Polignano a Mare

Polignano a Mare is a beautiful town located on the Adriatic Sea, and its clear waters are a must-visit for any traveler to Puglia. The town is known for its stunning cliffside location, perched on top of limestone cliffs that drop straight into the sea. Here's what you can expect when you take a dip in the crystal-clear waters of Polignano a Mare:

Swimming and Sunbathing
The beaches of Polignano a Mare are relatively small but offer an intimate and picturesque experience. The town has several small coves, including Lama Monachile, which is a popular destination for swimmers and sunbathers. The beach is flanked by tall limestone cliffs and has crystal-clear water, making it a beautiful place to relax and take a dip.

Snorkeling and Diving
The waters of Polignano a Mare are perfect for snorkeling and diving, thanks to their clear visibility and abundant marine life. The town's diving center offers several diving courses for both beginners and advanced divers. The underwater world is fascinating and beautiful, with a variety of fish and other sea creatures, as well as interesting rock formations and caves to explore.

Boat Tours
Another way to explore the beautiful waters of Polignano a Mare is by taking a boat tour. Several companies offer boat

tours that take visitors along the stunning coastline, with stops at hidden coves and beaches, as well as exploring sea caves and grottoes. A boat tour is a perfect way to see the beauty of the Adriatic Sea from a different perspective and take in the stunning scenery of Polignano a Mare.

If you're interested in exploring more of the coastline, there are several other beautiful beaches and coves to visit around Polignano a Mare. Here are some other notable spots:

Cala Paura: This small cove is located just a short walk from the town center and is a popular destination for both locals and tourists. The beach is surrounded by high cliffs and has crystal-clear water, making it a great place to swim and relax.

Porto Cavallo: This beach is located just south of Polignano a Mare and is accessible by car. It's a long, sandy beach that's perfect for a day of sunbathing, swimming, and beach games. There are several beach bars and restaurants along the coast where you can enjoy a cold drink or a snack.

Grotta Palazzese: This is a unique and exclusive dining experience that you don't want to miss. Located in a sea cave just outside of Polignano a Mare, the restaurant offers a beautiful view of the sea and serves delicious seafood and traditional Pugliese dishes. The restaurant is open from May to October and requires a reservation in advance.

San Vito: This beautiful beach is located just a short drive from Polignano a Mare and offers a long stretch of sandy shoreline, clear blue water, and stunning views of the Adriatic Sea. The beach is equipped with all the necessary facilities, including umbrellas, sunbeds, and showers.

Polignano a Mare and its surrounding coastline are full of beautiful beaches, coves, and unique experiences. Whether you're looking for a day of sunbathing, swimming, snorkeling, diving, or boat tours, you're sure to find something to suit your interests and preferences. Don't miss out on this breathtaking part of Puglia!

Relax on the Sandy Shores of Torre Lapillo

Torre Lapillo is a small seaside town located on the Ionian coast of Puglia. The town is famous for its long stretches of white sandy beaches and crystal-clear waters that make it a popular destination for beach lovers.

The beach in Torre Lapillo is divided into several small coves, each with its own unique charm. The water is shallow and calm, making it perfect for swimming and snorkeling. You can also rent umbrellas and sun loungers to relax and soak up the sun.

One of the most popular beaches in Torre Lapillo is the Spiaggia delle Dune, which is a long stretch of white sand surrounded by sand dunes. This beach is perfect for families with children as the water is shallow and there are many facilities such as restrooms, showers, and snack bars nearby.

If you're looking for a quieter spot, head to the Punta Prosciutto beach, which is a secluded cove surrounded by lush Mediterranean vegetation. The beach here is less crowded, and the water is incredibly clear, making it perfect for snorkeling and exploring the marine life.

In addition to sunbathing and swimming, there are many other activities to enjoy in Torre Lapillo. You can go windsurfing, paddleboarding, or take a boat trip to explore the nearby caves and grottoes. There are also many restaurants and cafes nearby where you can sample the local cuisine and enjoy a cold drink while watching the sunset over the sea.

In addition to the beach and water activities, Torre Lapillo also offers some interesting cultural attractions. One of the most notable is the Torre Lapillo Tower, a historic watchtower built in the 16th century to protect the town from pirate attacks. Today, the tower serves as a museum, providing visitors with a glimpse into the area's rich history and culture.

If you're interested in exploring more of the surrounding area, you can take a short drive to the nearby town of Porto Cesareo, which is home to several interesting historical sites and cultural attractions. You can visit the Porto Cesareo Archeological Museum, which showcases artifacts from the area's ancient Greek and Roman past, or explore the charming historic center of the town, with its narrow streets and traditional architecture.

Another popular destination near Torre Lapillo is the Punta Pizzo Nature Reserve, which offers visitors the opportunity to explore the area's natural beauty and wildlife. The reserve is home to a variety of plant and animal species, including migratory birds and rare plant species, and offers hiking trails and guided tours.

Admire the Natural Beauty of Gargano National Park

Gargano National Park is a beautiful and diverse national park located in the northern part of Puglia. With its stunning coastline, dense forests, and rugged mountains, the park is a paradise for nature lovers and outdoor enthusiasts.

The park's coastline is one of its most popular attractions, and for good reason. With its crystal-clear waters, hidden coves, and towering cliffs, the coastline offers some of the most beautiful scenery in the region. Visitors can explore the coast on foot or by boat, taking in the stunning views and soaking up the Mediterranean sun.

One of the most popular areas in the park is the Foresta Umbra, a dense forest that covers over 11,000 hectares. The forest is home to a variety of plant and animal species, including ancient oak trees, wild boar, and deer. Visitors can hike or bike through the forest, taking in the peaceful surroundings and admiring the natural beauty of the area.

The mountains of Gargano National Park are also worth exploring. With their rugged terrain and panoramic views, they offer a unique and challenging hiking experience for adventurous visitors. The highest peak in the park is Monte Calvo, which stands at 1,065 meters tall and offers stunning views of the surrounding landscape.

Gargano National Park is also home to a number of historic and cultural sites. The park is dotted with charming towns and villages that offer a glimpse into the region's rich history and culture. One such town is Vieste, a picturesque fishing village that boasts a beautiful old town and a stunning cathedral.

Gargano National Park can also explore a number of caves and grottoes, including the famous Grotta Pagliacci. This cave is known for its stunning stalactites and stalagmites, as well as its underground lake.

In addition to hiking and exploring the park's natural beauty, visitors can also take part in a variety of outdoor activities, such as mountain biking, horseback riding, and sea kayaking. The park's coastline is particularly popular for water sports such as windsurfing, kiteboarding, and snorkeling.

For those interested in history and culture, Gargano National Park offers a number of fascinating sites and monuments. The park is home to a number of ancient churches and monasteries, including the famous Abbey of Santa Maria di Pulsano, which dates back to the 11th century. The park is also home to a number of prehistoric and archaeological sites, such as the ancient village of San Felice and the dolmens of Monte Saraceno.

Chapter 3: History and Culture

Puglia is steeped in history and culture, with a rich heritage that spans thousands of years. In this chapter, we will explore some of the region's most fascinating historical and cultural attractions.

Wander the Streets of Alberobello's Trulli

Alberobello's Trulli are an iconic feature of Puglia's landscape and a must-see attraction for visitors to the region. These traditional dry-stone houses with conical roofs have been around since the 14th century and were originally built by farmers as temporary shelter. The trulli were constructed using a technique that involved stacking stone slabs without the use of mortar, making them resistant to earthquakes and allowing them to blend seamlessly into the surrounding countryside.

Today, Alberobello's trulli are a UNESCO World Heritage Site and a popular tourist attraction. The historic district of Alberobello is home to over 1,500 trulli, making it one of the largest concentrations of trulli in the region. Visitors can wander the narrow streets of the district and admire the unique architecture of the trulli up close. Many of the trulli have been converted into shops, restaurants, and museums, offering visitors the opportunity to learn more about the trulli's fascinating history and culture.

One of the most interesting aspects of the trulli is their interior design. Inside, the trulli are divided into different areas that serve different purposes, such as living spaces, storage areas, and animal shelters. The interior of the trulli is often decorated with intricate frescoes and traditional furnishings, giving visitors a glimpse into what life was like in rural Puglia centuries ago.

In addition to exploring the trulli themselves, visitors can also participate in guided tours that offer insights into the history and culture of the region. These tours typically include visits to historic landmarks such as the Church of Saint Anthony, which features a stunning collection of baroque art, and the Trullo Sovrano, the largest and most impressive trullo in Alberobello.

For those interested in learning more about the trulli's unique construction and cultural significance, there are several museums and workshops in Alberobello that offer educational experiences. The Trullo Sovrano Museum, for example, is a great place to start. This museum is housed inside a large trullo and offers visitors the opportunity to explore the interior of a trullo and learn about its history and construction.

Another popular museum is the Casa Pezzolla Museum, which is located in a cluster of trulli and features exhibits on traditional Puglian life and crafts. Visitors can see demonstrations of traditional weaving, embroidery, and pottery-making techniques, as well as learn about the role of agriculture and food production in Puglian culture.

In addition to exploring the trulli and museums, visitors can also sample some of the delicious local cuisine in Alberobello's many restaurants and cafes. Puglian cuisine is known for its use of fresh, locally sourced ingredients and its emphasis on simple, rustic flavors. Some popular dishes to try include orecchiette pasta with broccoli rabe and sausage, roasted meats such as lamb or pork, and a variety of fresh seafood dishes.

Visit the Historic Castle of Otranto

The Historic Castle of Otranto is a must-visit attraction in Puglia for anyone interested in history and culture. Built by the Aragonese in the 15th century, the castle played a vital role in defending the city of Otranto against Turkish invasion. It was designed to be a fortress, with thick walls, towers, and a moat that surrounded the castle.

The castle's history is fascinating, and visitors can learn about it through the museum exhibits that showcase its rich heritage. The museum has a collection of medieval artifacts and paintings, as well as exhibits that detail the castle's military history and its role in shaping the local culture.

One of the highlights of a visit to the castle is exploring the many rooms and galleries that are open to the public. Visitors can walk through the castle's impressive halls and chambers, admiring the intricate stonework and impressive architecture. The castle's ramparts offer stunning views of the surrounding city and countryside, providing a glimpse into the region's past and present.

The castle has been renovated and restored over the years, ensuring that it remains a well-preserved and significant historical site. It has been used for a variety of events, including concerts, exhibitions, and festivals, making it a lively and dynamic cultural center in the region.

In addition to its historical and cultural significance, the castle is also a popular destination for visitors due to its location in the heart of Otranto. The castle is situated within the city's historic center, which is home to many charming streets, alleys, and buildings that offer a glimpse into the city's past.

Visitors can also take a guided tour of the castle, which provides an in-depth look at the castle's history, architecture, and cultural significance. The knowledgeable guides provide interesting and informative commentary, making the tour a great way to learn more about the castle and the surrounding area.

One of the most striking features of the castle is its impressive exterior, with its imposing walls, towers, and drawbridge. Visitors can walk along the castle walls, which offer panoramic views of the city and the sea beyond. The castle's interior is equally impressive, with its soaring ceilings, grand staircases, and ornate decorations.

The castle has played a significant role in the history of the region, and visitors can learn about its many historical events and figures. For example, the castle was the site of a famous siege in 1480, when Turkish forces captured the city of Otranto and held it for several months before being driven out by the Venetians. The castle also played a role in the Italian Wars of Independence in the 19th century, when it was used as a military barracks.

In addition to its historical and cultural significance, the castle is also a popular venue for cultural events and activities. The castle hosts a variety of events throughout the year, including concerts, theater performances, and art exhibitions. These events provide a unique opportunity to experience the castle in a new way, and to appreciate its cultural importance in the region.

Marvel at the Baroque Architecture of Lecce

Lecce is a city in southern Italy that is known for its magnificent Baroque architecture, which is characterized by elaborate decorations and ornate designs. The city's historic center is a treasure trove of stunning Baroque buildings, including palaces, churches, and other important structures that are a testament to the region's rich cultural heritage.

One of the most famous buildings in Lecce is the Basilica di Santa Croce, which is considered a masterpiece of Baroque architecture. Built in the 17th century, the basilica is adorned with intricate carvings, sculptures, and reliefs that are sure to take your breath away. The façade alone is a work of art, featuring a complex interplay of light and shadow that creates a stunning visual effect.

Another iconic building in Lecce is the Palazzo dei Celestini, which was built in the early 16th century. The palace is known for its ornate balconies, elaborate carvings, and stunning frescoes that adorn its walls and ceilings. Visitors can also admire the palace's impressive courtyard, which is surrounded by elegant arches and decorated with beautiful statues.

Other notable Baroque buildings in Lecce include the Church of San Matteo, the Church of Santa Maria della Grazie, and the Piazza del Duomo, which is home to the city's impressive cathedral. As you wander through the winding streets and alleyways of Lecce's historic center, you will be transported back in time to a period of great artistic and cultural flourishing.

In addition to its stunning Baroque architecture, Lecce is also known for its vibrant cultural scene, which includes music, art, and theater. Throughout the year, the city plays host to a variety of cultural events and festivals, including the Lecce Baroque Festival, which celebrates the region's rich artistic heritage.

If you're a fan of architecture and history, a visit to Lecce is an absolute must. Take a leisurely stroll through the city's historic center and marvel at the intricate details of the Baroque buildings that line its streets. You're sure to be enchanted by the beauty and elegance of this magnificent city.

In addition to the Baroque architecture, Lecce also has a rich history that is reflected in the city's museums and historical sites. One of the most important of these is the Castle of Charles V, which was built in the 16th century and served as a military fortress for many years. Today, the castle houses the Museo Archeologico Provinciale, which features exhibits on the region's ancient history, including artifacts from the Greek and Roman periods.

Another important museum in Lecce is the Museo Diocesano, which is located in the Palazzo dei Vescovi. The museum features a collection of religious art and artifacts, including paintings, sculptures, and tapestries from the 17th and 18th centuries. Visitors can also admire the beautiful frescoes that adorn the ceilings and walls of the palazzo.

For a glimpse into daily life in Lecce during the Baroque period, visit the Palazzo Taurino, which is home to the Museum of the Papier-Mâché. The museum showcases the art of papier-mâché, which was a popular craft in Lecce during the 17th and 18th centuries. Visitors can learn about the techniques used to create these beautiful works of art, and admire the intricate details of the objects on display.

Aside from the museums, Lecce also has several important historical sites that are worth visiting. One of these is the Roman Amphitheater, which dates back to the 2nd century AD and could seat up to 25,000 spectators. Visitors can walk through the remains of the amphitheater and imagine what it must have been like to attend a gladiatorial contest or other public spectacle.

Explore the Roman Ruins of Egnazia

The Roman Ruins of Egnazia are a must-visit destination for history enthusiasts and archaeology buffs. Egnazia was an important Roman city that played a vital role in the region's commercial and political affairs during ancient times. The city was strategically located on the Adriatic coast, which enabled it to become a vital port and a hub of maritime trade and commerce.

Visitors to Egnazia can explore the ruins of the ancient city, which date back to the 4th century BC. The most notable feature of the ruins is the Roman amphitheater, which is one of the largest and most impressive in southern Italy. The amphitheater was used for various forms of entertainment, including gladiator fights, animal hunts, and theatrical performances.

In addition to the amphitheater, visitors can also explore the remains of the port, which was once a bustling hub of maritime activity. The port was the primary gateway for goods and commodities that were transported to and from other parts of the Mediterranean. It was also a key military outpost for the Roman Empire, as it provided strategic access to the Adriatic Sea.

Other notable ruins in Egnazia include the many temples and public buildings that have been uncovered in recent years. These include the remains of a temple dedicated to the goddess Venus, a public bath complex, and several Roman villas that were once home to the city's wealthy elite.

Visitors to Egnazia can also learn more about the history and culture of the ancient city at the onsite museum. The museum features an extensive collection of artifacts, including ancient coins, pottery, and sculpture, that provide insights into life in Egnazia during ancient times.

The site of Egnazia is vast, covering approximately 10 hectares, and there is much more to explore beyond the main attractions. Visitors can take a walk through the city's old streets and get a sense of what life was like for the people who once lived there. Some of the old walls and gates of the city still stand, providing a glimpse into the defensive measures that were taken during ancient times.

One of the most interesting aspects of Egnazia is the way in which the city has been preserved over the centuries. The site was abandoned after the fall of the Roman Empire and remained largely untouched until the early 20th century. As a result, much of the ancient city has been remarkably well-preserved, giving visitors a unique glimpse into the past.

Another fascinating aspect of Egnazia is the way in which it has been studied and excavated over the years. The first archaeological excavations of the site began in the 20th century, and they have continued up to the present day. As a result, visitors to Egnazia can witness ongoing excavations and learn about the latest discoveries in the field of archaeology.

Chapter 4: Outdoor Activities

Puglia is a great destination for outdoor enthusiasts, offering a variety of activities to enjoy. From hiking and biking to scuba diving and kitesurfing, there is something for everyone.

Hike the Ravines of Matera

The ravines near Matera provide a unique hiking experience for visitors to the area. The Gravina di Matera, also known as the Canyon of Matera, is a natural gorge that cuts through the city and offers stunning views of the surrounding landscape. This deep canyon is an impressive geological feature and has been carved out over millions of years by the flow of water.

Hiking the ravines of Matera allows visitors to explore the rugged terrain, winding paths, and rocky landscapes of the area. Along the way, hikers will encounter natural springs, waterfalls, and wildlife such as eagles and foxes. The flora of the ravines includes species like Mediterranean scrub, Aleppo pines, holm oaks, and carob trees.

The hike is not too strenuous, but it does require a bit of physical fitness and good footwear. There are several well-marked trails that vary in difficulty, and hikers can choose to take a guided tour or explore the ravines on their own. Some popular hiking routes include the Pulo di Altamura, which takes hikers to a scenic plateau overlooking the Gravina di Matera, and the Grotta del pipistrello, which is a cave with interesting rock formations and bats.

For those interested in history, the ravines of Matera also offer a glimpse into the ancient past of the region. The rock-hewn churches, monasteries, and settlements located within the ravines are a testament to the area's long and fascinating history.

Additionally, hiking in the ravines of Matera can be a great way to escape the crowds and experience a more tranquil side of the city. While Matera itself can be quite busy and bustling with tourists, the ravines provide a peaceful and serene setting for hikers to explore.

One of the most popular hiking routes is the "Parco della Murgia Materana," which is a vast natural park that covers over 8,000 hectares of land. This park includes several hiking trails that wind through the ravines and offer stunning views of the surrounding countryside. Along the way, hikers can stop at various viewpoints to take in the impressive rock formations and vistas.

Another popular route is the "Gravina di Picciano," which is a narrow canyon that runs through the heart of Matera. This hike is a bit more challenging than some of the others, as it involves climbing steep rocks and traversing narrow paths. However, the stunning views and unique terrain make it well worth the effort.

In addition to hiking, visitors to the ravines of Matera can also enjoy other outdoor activities such as rock climbing and canyoning. These activities provide an even more thrilling way to explore the rugged terrain of the area.

Bike Along the Apulian Aqueduct Cycle Path

The Apulian Aqueduct Cycle Path is a must-do activity for anyone visiting Puglia who loves to bike and explore the region's rural landscape. The cycle path stretches for 37 kilometers along the ancient aqueduct, which once provided water to the city of Brindisi during the Roman era.

Starting from the town of Torre Santa Susanna, the trail meanders through the rolling countryside of Puglia, passing through charming villages, olive groves, vineyards, and fields of wheat. Along the way, there are several points of interest to stop and explore, such as the San Vito dei Normanni Castle, the Church of Santa Maria degli Angeli, and the Monumental Olive Tree of Cellino San Marco, which is over 2000 years old.

The trail is relatively flat and suitable for cyclists of all levels. The path is well-maintained, with clear signs marking the route and regular rest areas where cyclists can stop to take a break or enjoy a picnic. The route is also well-shaded, with trees lining the path and providing relief from the sun.

For those who don't have their own bike, there are several rental options available in the area, and some guided tours that offer the opportunity to explore the area with a local guide. The cycle path can be completed in a single day, but many people choose to take their time and stop overnight in one of the charming towns along the way, such as San Michele Salentino or Mesagne.

There are several other things to keep in mind before embarking on the Apulian Aqueduct Cycle Path. Firstly, it's important to wear appropriate clothing and footwear for biking, such as comfortable shorts, a lightweight shirt, and sturdy closed-toe shoes. A helmet is also recommended for safety.

Secondly, it's a good idea to bring along some snacks and drinks to keep your energy levels up during the ride. There are plenty of small cafes and restaurants along the way where you can stop for a coffee, a gelato, or a bite to eat, but it's always good to have some provisions on hand in case you get hungry or thirsty.

Lastly, it's important to respect the environment and local communities along the way. This means not littering, sticking to the designated trail, and being mindful of other cyclists and pedestrians on the path. It's also a good idea to learn a few basic Italian phrases, as not everyone in the rural areas of Puglia speaks English.

Go Scuba Diving in Santa Maria di Leuca

Scuba diving in Santa Maria di Leuca is a must-do activity for anyone who loves to explore the underwater world. The town, located at the southernmost tip of the Salento peninsula, boasts some of the clearest waters in the Mediterranean, with visibility often exceeding 30 meters.

The marine life in Santa Maria di Leuca is abundant and varied, with many species of fish, crustaceans, and mollusks to be found. Divers can expect to see octopuses, groupers, moray eels, and even the occasional dolphin or turtle.

One of the main attractions of scuba diving in Santa Maria di Leuca is the underwater caves and grottoes. The area is known for its karst formations, which have created a network of tunnels and caverns beneath the sea. Some of the most famous dive sites in the area include the Grotta del Diavolo (Devil's Cave), the Grotta del Presepe (Nativity Cave), and the Grotta del Ciolo.

For those who are new to scuba diving, there are several diving centers in Santa Maria di Leuca that offer courses and training programs. These centers have experienced instructors who can teach the necessary skills and safety procedures, so that even beginners can enjoy the underwater world. For more experienced divers, there are plenty of challenging dive sites to explore, with depths ranging from 10 to 40 meters.

Additionally, scuba diving in Santa Maria di Leuca can be enjoyed all year round. However, the best time to dive is during the summer months when the water temperature is at its warmest, usually reaching 25-28°C. During the winter months, the water temperature can drop to around 14-16°C, which is still suitable for diving, but a wetsuit is necessary to keep warm.

Apart from scuba diving, there are other water activities that visitors can enjoy in Santa Maria di Leuca. Snorkeling is a great option for those who want to explore the underwater world without the need for scuba equipment. The clear waters of Santa Maria di Leuca make it easy to see a variety of marine life even with just a snorkel and mask.

For those who want to stay above water, there are also boat tours available that take visitors along the coast and to nearby grottoes and coves. These tours offer a different perspective of the coastline and allow visitors to see the natural beauty of the area from a unique vantage point.

Experience the Thrill of Kitesurfing in Otranto

Kitesurfing is an exciting and challenging sport that involves using a kite to pull a rider on a board across the water. Otranto, located on the eastern coast of Puglia, offers ideal conditions for kitesurfing, with consistent winds and calm waters.

The best time to go kitesurfing in Otranto is from May to September, when the winds are strongest and the weather is warm. During this time, you can expect winds of around 20 knots and temperatures in the mid-20s Celsius (mid-70s Fahrenheit).

There are several kitesurfing schools in Otranto that offer lessons and equipment rental for beginners and experienced kitesurfers. Some of the most popular schools include Otranto Surf Center, Kitesurf Salento, and Kitesurf Point.

Lessons typically start with an introduction to the equipment and safety procedures, followed by some basic skills such as controlling the kite and body dragging. Once you have mastered these skills, you can progress to riding the board and performing tricks.

In addition to kitesurfing, Otranto offers a range of other water sports such as windsurfing, paddleboarding, and kayaking. The town itself is also worth exploring, with its charming historic center, ancient castle, and beautiful beaches.

When it comes to kitesurfing in Otranto, it's important to note that there are designated areas for the activity, marked by buoys. These areas are located away from the swimming beaches and boat traffic, ensuring a safe and enjoyable experience for all.

One of the advantages of taking kitesurfing lessons in Otranto is that the schools provide all the necessary equipment, including kites, boards, and wetsuits. This means that you don't have to invest in your own gear if you're just starting out.

In addition to the schools, there are also a number of kitesurfing shops in Otranto where you can purchase gear if you decide to continue with the sport after your lessons.

It's worth noting that kitesurfing can be a physically demanding sport, so it's important to be in good physical shape and have some experience with other board sports such as skateboarding, snowboarding, or wakeboarding.

Chapter 5: Festivals and Events

Puglia is known for its vibrant festivals and events throughout the year, showcasing the region's rich history, culture, and traditions. Whether you're a music lover, foodie, or simply looking for a unique cultural experience, Puglia has something to offer for everyone.

Celebrate the Feast of St. Nicholas in Bari

The Feast of St. Nicholas, or "Festa di San Nicola," is one of the most important events in the city of Bari, held every year on December 6th. The festival celebrates the life and legacy of St. Nicholas, the patron saint of the city and the inspiration for the modern-day Santa Claus.

The festival starts with a solemn religious ceremony in the Basilica of St. Nicholas, where the relics of the saint are kept. The ceremony is attended by thousands of locals and visitors who come to pay their respects and participate in the festivities.

After the religious ceremony, a grand procession takes place through the streets of Bari, featuring a statue of St. Nicholas carried on the shoulders of a group of "pittari," or porters, dressed in traditional white robes and red sashes. The procession is accompanied by a brass band and local folk groups, who perform traditional music and dances along the way.

As the procession makes its way through the city, locals decorate their balconies and windows with red and white ribbons, the colors of St. Nicholas. The atmosphere is lively and festive, with vendors selling traditional foods and drinks along the streets.

The highlight of the festival is the spectacular fireworks display that takes place over the seafront, attracting thousands of spectators. The fireworks show is accompanied by live music and is a true spectacle, reflecting the joy and excitement of the festival.

Visitors to Bari during the Feast of St. Nicholas can also enjoy local delicacies such as "cartellate," a sweet pastry dessert, and "sgagliozze," fried polenta slices. The festival offers a unique opportunity to experience the city's rich cultural heritage and join in the celebration of one of its most beloved patron saints.

In addition to the procession, fireworks, and local foods, there are other events and activities to enjoy during the Feast of St. Nicholas in Bari. For instance, there are often exhibitions and performances highlighting the art and culture of Puglia. These events may take place in the streets, town squares, or museums and galleries.

One of the most interesting things about the Feast of St. Nicholas is the opportunity to witness the centuries-old tradition of the "blessing of the sea." This ritual takes place early in the morning of December 6th, when the Archbishop of Bari boards a boat and sails out to sea. He blesses the water with holy water, and local fishermen throw wreaths into the water in honor of St. Nicholas. This ceremony is a reminder of the importance of the sea to the people of Bari, who have long relied on fishing and seafaring for their livelihood.

The Feast of St. Nicholas is a family-friendly event, with activities and entertainment suitable for people of all ages. Children will be especially delighted by the atmosphere of excitement and joy, as well as the chance to meet the man who inspired Santa Claus.

Attend the Taranta Music Festival in Salento

The Taranta Music Festival, also known as the La Notte della Taranta, is an annual music festival held in the Salento region of Puglia in August. It celebrates the traditional music of Puglia known as pizzica and has become one of the most popular festivals in Italy, attracting visitors from all over the world.

The festival usually lasts for about two weeks, with concerts and events taking place in different towns and villages throughout the Salento peninsula. The highlight of the festival is the final concert, which is held in the town of Melpignano and broadcast live on Italian television.

The festival features a variety of musical performances, including traditional folk music, world music, and contemporary interpretations of pizzica. Visitors can expect to see artists playing traditional instruments like the tambourine, accordion, and violin, as well as contemporary instruments like the guitar and electric bass.

In addition to the music, the festival also offers workshops, dance lessons, and cultural events. Visitors can participate in traditional dance classes, learn about local history and traditions, and sample local food and wine.

One of the most popular events during the festival is the "tarantella" dance, which is a fast-paced dance that dates back to the 17th century. The dance is said to have originated as a cure for the "tarantula bite," a condition believed to cause fever and delirium. Today, the dance is a celebration of local culture and is performed throughout the festival.

Additionally, the festival provides an opportunity to experience the rich cultural heritage of Salento and the surrounding areas. Visitors can witness the unique blend of Greek, Roman, and Byzantine influences that have shaped the region's history and culture over the centuries.

The festival's atmosphere is vibrant and energetic, with people of all ages coming together to dance, sing, and celebrate. The streets are filled with colorful costumes, traditional food and drink, and a sense of joy and excitement that is infectious.

It is worth noting that the Taranta Music Festival is not just a tourist attraction, but a significant cultural event for the people of Puglia. The festival plays an important role in preserving and promoting the region's traditional music and dance, which is an integral part of the local identity.

Experience the Carnival of Putignano

The Carnival of Putignano is one of the oldest and most famous carnivals in Italy, dating back to the 1400s. It takes place in the town of Putignano, located in the province of Bari, and is a true spectacle of colors, music, and traditions. The carnival takes place on Sundays and Tuesdays from January 17 to February 28, with the highlight being the last weekend of the carnival.

The carnival is a celebration of the end of winter and the beginning of spring, and it features colorful parades with floats and costumed performers, as well as music, dancing, and street performances. The parade starts in the town's main square, Piazza Plebiscito, and winds through the town's historic center, where visitors can enjoy the vibrant atmosphere and admire the intricate floats and costumes.

During the carnival, visitors can also sample local delicacies, such as "frittelle," a type of fried doughnut, and "pettole," fried dough balls filled with anchovies or tomato sauce. Local wine and "taralli," a type of savory biscuit, are also popular treats to enjoy during the festivities.

The carnival has its own unique character, and each year the theme of the carnival changes, with floats and costumes designed accordingly. The floats are often satirical and depict famous figures or current events, making the carnival a fun and engaging commentary on contemporary society.

In addition to the parades and food, the carnival also features live music performances, theater shows, and art exhibitions, making it a diverse and dynamic event for visitors of all ages. The atmosphere is lively and festive, with people of all backgrounds and nationalities coming together to celebrate the carnival.

One of the most exciting moments of the Carnival of Putignano is the "battle of confetti." During this event, the crowd is split into two teams and throws confetti at each other, creating a colorful and joyous moment that is sure to bring a smile to everyone's face.

Another highlight of the carnival is the "Festa della Candelora," which takes place on February 2nd, and marks the halfway point of the carnival. During this event, the parade features a special candle, which is lit in honor of the Madonna and Child, and carried through the streets of the town.

Visitors to the Carnival of Putignano can also take part in various workshops and activities, such as mask-making or costume design, allowing them to fully immerse themselves in the local culture and traditions.

The Carnival of Putignano is a true celebration of life and culture, offering a unique and unforgettable experience for visitors to Puglia. With its vibrant parades, delicious food, and diverse entertainment, the carnival is a must-see event that is sure to delight and inspire all who attend. Whether you're a seasoned traveler or visiting Puglia for the first time, be sure to add the Carnival of Putignano to your itinerary and experience the magic and joy of this unforgettable event.

Watch the Festa di San Pardo Horse Race in Galatina

The Festa di San Pardo is an annual festival held in the town of Galatina, located in the Salento region of Puglia. The festival takes place in honor of Saint Pardo, the town's patron saint. The festival is held over several days, with the highlight being a horse race that takes place in the historic center of the town.

The horse race is a unique and exciting event that has been a tradition in Galatina for centuries. The race is held on a course that winds through the narrow streets of the town's historic center. The course is approximately 1 kilometer long and features tight turns and steep inclines, making it a challenging and thrilling race for the riders.

The race itself is a bareback competition, with riders from different parts of Puglia competing for the honor of being the champion of the Festa di San Pardo. The riders must navigate the course at high speeds, weaving in and out of the crowds of spectators who line the streets to watch the race.

The horse race is just one part of the Festa di San Pardo, which also includes live music, food, and drink. Visitors to the festival can sample local delicacies, such as "pittule," a type of fried dough ball, and "pettole," fried dough balls filled with anchovies or tomato sauce. There are also traditional music performances, street performers, and other entertainment throughout the festival.

The Festa di San Pardo is not only a thrilling and entertaining event, but it also has deep roots in the history and culture of Galatina. The festival is said to have originated in the 15th century, when the town was under attack from the Ottoman Empire. The legend goes that Saint Pardo appeared on horseback and led the townspeople to victory, and the horse race is held every year in honor of this event.

The festival has evolved over the centuries, but it has remained an important part of Galatina's cultural identity. The horse race is not just a competition but also a symbol of unity and community spirit. The riders and horses come from different parts of Puglia, but they all come together to celebrate the rich history and culture of the region.

If you're planning to attend the Festa di San Pardo, there are a few things to keep in mind. The festival typically takes place in late May or early June, so be sure to check the exact dates before you make your travel plans. The horse race itself is a popular event, so be prepared for large crowds and limited seating. It's also a good idea to arrive early to get a good spot along the course.

Chapter 6: Shopping and Markets

Puglia is a region renowned for its culinary traditions, producing some of the freshest and most delicious food in Italy. Shopping for local produce, pottery, and other handicrafts is an excellent way to experience the region's unique culture and support local businesses.

Browse the Local Produce at Bari's Mercato Coperto

Bari's Mercato Coperto, also known as the Covered Market or Mercato del Borgo Antico, is a bustling indoor market located in the historic center of Bari. The market is a popular destination for locals and tourists alike, and it's the perfect place to shop for fresh, locally-sourced ingredients for a picnic or a homemade meal.

As you enter the market, you'll be greeted by the vibrant colors and aromas of fresh produce, including fruits, vegetables, herbs, and spices. You'll also find a wide range of meats, including lamb, beef, and pork, as well as cured meats like prosciutto, salami, and capocollo. If you're a seafood lover, you'll be delighted by the selection of fresh fish and seafood, including octopus, squid, shrimp, and anchovies.

The market also has an excellent selection of cheeses, including fresh ricotta, creamy burrata, and tangy pecorino. You'll also find a variety of olives, nuts, and dried fruits, perfect for snacking or adding to your homemade meals.

In addition to food items, the market has several stalls selling local wines, olive oils, and other specialty products, like homemade pasta and sauces. You can also find handmade baskets, pottery, and other souvenirs that make perfect gifts or keepsakes.

Bari's Mercato Coperto is open daily, from early morning until late afternoon, making it easy to fit a visit into your itinerary. Whether you're looking for ingredients for a picnic, a special meal, or just want to experience the vibrant atmosphere of a bustling local market, the Mercato Coperto is the perfect destination.

Aside from shopping, there are many other things to enjoy at the Mercato Coperto. The market is a great place to people-watch, with locals doing their daily shopping and vendors haggling over prices. You can also engage with the friendly vendors and learn more about the products they're selling, the best ways to prepare them, and the history behind them.

If you're feeling hungry, there are several food stalls and cafes within the market where you can sample local specialties like panzerotti, a type of savory turnover filled with cheese and tomato sauce, or pasticciotto, a traditional pastry filled with custard or cream.

During the summer months, the market can get quite crowded, so it's best to arrive early in the morning to beat the crowds. However, even during the busiest times, the market retains its lively and convivial atmosphere, with the vendors shouting out their wares and the customers bargaining for the best deals.

Overall, a visit to Bari's Mercato Coperto is a must for anyone visiting the region. It's a great place to experience the local culture, sample fresh and delicious foods, and pick up some unique souvenirs to take home.

Shop for Handmade Pottery in Grottaglie

Grottaglie, located in the Taranto province of Puglia, has a long-standing tradition of ceramic production that dates back to the 16th century. The town is famous for its unique style of ceramics known as "Grottaglie ceramics," which are characterized by their vibrant colors, intricate designs, and high-quality craftsmanship.

In Grottaglie, you can visit the local shops and boutiques to shop for handmade pottery, including dishes, vases, decorative items, and even sculptures. These pieces make great souvenirs or gifts to take home. You can also find a variety of traditional and modern designs to suit your tastes.

One of the unique experiences in Grottaglie is the opportunity to visit the workshops and see how the pottery is made. Many of the workshops are still family-owned and operated, passed down from generation to generation. You can watch the artisans at work, throwing clay on the wheel, painting designs by hand, and firing the pieces in kilns.

Visiting Grottaglie's workshops is a chance to witness the traditional ceramic-making process and learn about the history and techniques that have been passed down for centuries. You can also purchase ceramics directly from the workshops, often at lower prices than you would find in the shops.

In addition to shopping for pottery, Grottaglie is a charming town with a beautiful historic center to explore. You can walk through the narrow streets, admire the old buildings, and enjoy a meal or drink at one of the local restaurants or cafes.

Another interesting aspect of Grottaglie's ceramic tradition is the town's famous ceramic district. The district is home to over 50 ceramic workshops, making it one of the largest concentrations of ceramic production in Italy. The district is also a protected cultural heritage site and has been recognized as an important center of Italian craftsmanship.

If you're interested in learning more about Grottaglie's ceramics, you can also visit the Museo delle Ceramiche, a museum dedicated to the town's ceramic history. The museum showcases a collection of Grottaglie ceramics dating back to the 16th century, as well as works by contemporary artists. It's an excellent place to learn more about the town's artistic heritage and see some of the most beautiful and unique pieces of Grottaglie ceramics.

In addition to the traditional Grottaglie ceramics, many contemporary artists are also creating innovative and unique ceramic pieces, pushing the boundaries of traditional ceramic-making techniques. You can find these pieces in some of the town's more modern shops and galleries, as well as in some of the workshops.

Visit the Weekly Market in Ostuni

Ostuni's weekly market is one of the most vibrant and colorful places to shop in Puglia. Held every Saturday in the historic center of the town, the market attracts locals and tourists alike who come to browse the many stalls selling local products and handicrafts.

One of the highlights of the market is the fresh produce, including a wide range of olives, cheeses, and bread. The region is known for its olive groves, and you can sample a variety of different olives, including the popular Cerignola olive, which is one of the largest and tastiest olives in the world. Cheeses such as burrata, pecorino, and caciocavallo are also popular items, and you can often see the cheese being made right in front of you.

In addition to food, the market is also an excellent place to shop for handicrafts such as baskets and leather goods. Local artisans sell their wares at the market, and you can find handmade baskets, bags, and other accessories made from natural materials such as straw and leather.

The market is set in the historic center of Ostuni, surrounded by the town's iconic white-washed buildings, which make it a particularly picturesque place to shop. The streets are narrow, winding, and filled with the sounds and smells of the market, creating a vibrant and lively atmosphere.

The market in Ostuni is also an ideal place to pick up some unique and authentic souvenirs to take home with you. You can find a range of local handicrafts and artisanal products that make perfect gifts for friends and family or a reminder of your trip to Puglia.

Aside from food and handicrafts, the market also sells clothing, shoes, and accessories. You can find everything from vintage clothing and handmade shoes to trendy hats and jewelry. If you're in the market for some new additions to your wardrobe, the market is definitely worth a visit.

In addition to shopping, the market is also a great place to immerse yourself in the local culture and interact with the locals. You'll have the opportunity to chat with vendors and other shoppers, practice your Italian language skills, and learn more about the region's history and traditions.

It's worth noting that the market can get quite busy, especially during the summer months when tourists flock to the region. If you're looking to avoid the crowds, it's best to visit the market early in the morning or later in the afternoon.

Find Unique Souvenirs in Monopoli's Historic Center

Monopoli's historic center is a charming area full of narrow streets, ancient buildings, and small shops that offer a variety of unique items. The shops and boutiques in Monopoli sell an array of handmade crafts and souvenirs, including hand-painted ceramics, intricate jewelry, and handcrafted leather goods. The town has a long history of producing ceramics and pottery, and many of the items sold in the shops are made by local artisans using traditional techniques.

One of the must-visit shops in Monopoli is the ceramic workshop of Giuseppe Dalfino, who is renowned for his intricate and delicate pottery. Dalfino's workshop produces a wide range of items, from plates and vases to decorative sculptures, all with unique designs and colors. Visitors can also watch the craftsmen at work and learn more about the pottery-making process.

In addition to the ceramics, Monopoli's historic center is also home to many small bakeries and pastry shops that sell traditional sweets and pastries. One of the most famous is Pasticceria Martinucci, which has been making delicious pastries for over 50 years. The shop sells a wide variety of sweet treats, including the local favorite, "calzone di San Leonardo," a sweet pastry filled with ricotta cheese, almonds, and candied fruit.

Monopoli's historic center also offers many opportunities to shop for handcrafted leather goods, such as bags, belts, and wallets. The town has a long tradition of leatherworking, and many of the shops in the area sell high-quality, handmade leather goods.

Visitors to Monopoli's historic center can also find a variety of other unique and locally made items in the shops and boutiques. One popular item is the local olive oil, which is produced in the region and is considered some of the best in Italy. Many shops sell bottles of high-quality olive oil, along with other local products like dried pasta, cheeses, and wines.

For those looking for something truly special, Monopoli's historic center also offers a range of artisanal products, such as handmade jewelry, scarves, and clothing. The shops in the area often source their materials locally, and the pieces are made with care and attention to detail. Visitors can find one-of-a-kind items that make for great souvenirs or gifts for loved ones back home.

Aside from the shopping, visitors to Monopoli's historic center can also enjoy the beautiful architecture and historic landmarks. The town is home to a variety of churches and palaces, including the Baroque-style Cathedral of Madonna della Madia, which features stunning frescoes and artwork. Walking through the town's streets is like stepping back in time, with many of the buildings dating back hundreds of years.

Chapter 7: Hidden Gems

While Puglia has many popular attractions that draw crowds of tourists each year, there are also plenty of hidden gems to discover. From abandoned villages to underground caves, these hidden gems offer a unique and often overlooked perspective on the region's history and natural beauty.

Explore the Abandoned Village of Craco

Craco is a medieval village located in the province of Matera, about 50 km southwest of the city of Matera. The village is perched on a hilltop, offering stunning views of the surrounding countryside. The village was founded in the 8th century and has a rich history, having been ruled by various lords and feudal families over the centuries.

In the 20th century, Craco was hit by a series of landslides and earthquakes that forced its inhabitants to abandon the village in the 1960s. Today, the village is a popular destination for tourists, history buffs, and photographers who come to explore its abandoned streets and buildings.

Visitors can wander through the village's narrow alleys and staircases, admiring the crumbling buildings and imagining what life must have been like in this once-thriving community. Many of the buildings have been left untouched since the village was abandoned, providing a fascinating insight into the past.

One of the most striking buildings in the village is the Norman Tower, which dates back to the 11th century. The tower offers stunning views of the surrounding countryside and is a popular spot for photographers.

Craco has also been used as a film location for a number of movies, including "The Passion of the Christ" and "Quantum of Solace". The village's eerie atmosphere and historic charm make it a popular location for filmmakers.

Visitors should note that access to the village is restricted and guided tours are required. However, the tours offer a fascinating insight into the history of the village and are well worth the visit.

The guided tours of Craco usually begin at the entrance of the village, where visitors can see the remains of the ancient city walls and gate. The tour then takes visitors through the deserted streets of the village, passing by the ruins of the old castle, the church, and the historic houses.

As visitors walk through the village, they will notice the unique architecture of the buildings, which is a blend of Gothic, Renaissance, and Baroque styles. The buildings are made of local stone and have arched windows, balconies, and decorative cornices.

One of the most intriguing features of Craco is the underground crypt beneath the church. The crypt is a maze of tunnels and chambers that were used as burial sites by the villagers. Visitors can explore the crypt, which has been left untouched since the village was abandoned.

As well as the guided tours, there are also a number of events held in Craco throughout the year, including music concerts, theater performances, and art exhibitions. These events bring the village to life and offer visitors the chance to experience its unique atmosphere.

Discover the Underground Caves of Castellana Grotte

The Castellana Grotte is one of the most impressive underground cave systems in Italy, located in the province of Bari. This cave system is a natural masterpiece created by millions of years of erosion of limestone rock, resulting in intricate patterns and shapes that are a testament to the power of nature.

Guided tours are available for visitors who want to explore the various chambers and passageways of the caves. These tours offer a chance to witness the stunning beauty of the caves up close and personal. A knowledgeable guide will lead visitors through the system, pointing out the different rock formations and explaining how they were created.

The first part of the tour takes visitors through the "graveyard of the stalactites," a section of the caves where many stalactites have fallen over time and now litter the ground like tombstones. The guide will explain the formation of these structures, which are created by the slow drip of water over thousands of years.

Further along the tour, visitors will come across the "white cave," which is named for the white color of the stalactites and stalagmites. The formations here are especially delicate and intricate, and visitors will be awed by the natural beauty on display.

As the tour continues, visitors will come across several other chambers, each with its own unique features and formations. The highlight of the tour is the "grotta bianca" or the "white cave," which is considered one of the most beautiful chambers in the entire cave system.

It's important to note that the Castellana Grotte is a protected natural area, and visitors are required to follow certain rules and regulations to help preserve the cave system. For example, touching the formations is strictly prohibited, as even the slightest touch can damage the delicate structures that have taken millions of years to form. Additionally, visitors are required to stay on the designated paths during the tour, as wandering off-trail can cause damage to the cave floor and disturb the natural ecosystem.

One of the most unique features of the Castellana Grotte is the "Tarantula Cave," which is named for the large number of tarantulas that inhabit the cave. These spiders are not dangerous to humans and are actually considered an important part of the cave ecosystem, as they help control the insect population.

The tour of the Castellana Grotte lasts approximately 1.5 hours, and visitors should be prepared for some physical activity, as there are some steep inclines and uneven terrain. However, the stunning natural beauty of the cave system is well worth the effort, and the experience of exploring the underground world of the Castellana Grotte is truly unforgettable.

In addition to the guided tours of the caves, visitors can also enjoy the surrounding area, which is home to a number of restaurants, cafes, and shops. There is also a small museum located at the entrance to the cave system, where visitors can learn more about the geology and history of the Castellana Grotte.

Relax at the Thermal Baths of Santa Cesarea Terme

The town of Santa Cesarea Terme, located on the eastern coast of Puglia, is a popular destination for those seeking relaxation and rejuvenation. The town is famous for its thermal baths, which have been used for their healing properties for centuries. The thermal waters in Santa Cesarea Terme are rich in minerals such as sulfur, sodium, and magnesium, which are believed to have a variety of health benefits.

The thermal baths in Santa Cesarea Terme offer visitors the chance to soak in warm waters and indulge in a range of spa treatments. The waters are said to be particularly beneficial for those suffering from skin conditions, respiratory problems, and joint pain. The thermal baths also offer a range of treatments, including massages, mud baths, and aromatherapy.

In addition to the thermal baths, visitors to Santa Cesarea Terme can explore the town's many spas and wellness centers. These centers offer a range of treatments and services, including hydrotherapy, saunas, and Turkish baths. Many of the spas also offer yoga and meditation classes, as well as healthy eating options.

The town of Santa Cesarea Terme is also a great place to explore the surrounding countryside. The town is located on the Salento peninsula, which is known for its beautiful beaches and crystal-clear waters. Visitors can take a boat trip along the coast or explore the nearby nature reserve of Porto Selvaggio.

The thermal baths of Santa Cesarea Terme are not only a great place to relax and unwind, but they also have a rich history. The town has been a popular destination for those seeking the healing properties of the thermal waters since ancient times. The baths were even mentioned in Pliny the Elder's Naturalis Historia, a famous Roman encyclopedia written in the 1st century AD.

In the Middle Ages, the town was under the control of the Byzantine Empire and became an important center for the production of ceramics. The town's thermal baths continued to be a popular destination for travelers seeking the healing properties of the thermal waters.

Today, the thermal baths of Santa Cesarea Terme continue to attract visitors from all over the world. The town has a range of accommodations, from luxury hotels to more affordable guesthouses. Many of the hotels have their own thermal baths and spa facilities, making it easy for visitors to relax and rejuvenate in comfort.

In addition to the thermal baths, Santa Cesarea Terme has a range of other attractions. Visitors can explore the town's beautiful architecture, which includes elegant villas, historic churches, and colorful mosaics. The town is also famous for its seafood, with many restaurants serving delicious local dishes made with fresh fish and shellfish.

Visit the Coastal Village of Polignano a Mare

Polignano a Mare is a beautiful coastal town located on the Adriatic Sea in the province of Bari. While it is not necessarily a hidden gem, it is often overlooked by visitors who tend to stick to the more well-known destinations in

Puglia, such as Alberobello and Lecce. However, those who do make the journey to Polignano a Mare are rewarded with a picturesque and charming town that offers a range of activities and attractions.

The town is perched on a rocky cliff that overlooks the sea, making it an ideal destination for those who love stunning coastal scenery. Visitors can stroll along the town's narrow streets, which are lined with whitewashed houses, cafes, and shops. The old town is particularly charming, with its winding alleyways and historic architecture.

One of the main attractions in Polignano a Mare is the seafront promenade, which offers stunning views of the Adriatic Sea. Visitors can relax on the beach, take a dip in the crystal-clear waters, or simply enjoy the scenery. For those who are feeling adventurous, there are also a number of sea caves and grottoes to explore.

Foodies will also love Polignano a Mare, as the town is known for its seafood restaurants. Visitors can sample fresh seafood dishes, such as grilled octopus and fried anchovies, while enjoying the sea views. The town is also home to a number of gelato shops, where visitors can indulge in creamy and delicious gelato in a variety of flavors.

Additionally, Polignano a Mare has a rich cultural heritage and history that can be explored through its various landmarks and monuments. One of the most prominent landmarks in the town is the Romanesque church of Santa Maria Assunta, which dates back to the 11th century. The church is known for its beautiful rose window and Baroque altar, and is a popular destination for visitors interested in art and architecture.

Another popular attraction in Polignano a Mare is the statue of Domenico Modugno, the famous Italian singer and songwriter who wrote the hit song "Volare". The statue is located on the seafront promenade and is a popular spot for taking photos.

For those who are interested in history, the town also has a small archaeological museum that showcases artifacts from the prehistoric, Greek, and Roman periods.

Polignano a Mare offers a wonderful mix of natural beauty, history, and culture. It is a destination that should not be missed by those who are visiting Puglia and want to experience the best that this region has to offer. Whether you're interested in stunning coastal views, delicious food, or exploring the town's cultural heritage, Polignano a Mare has something for everyone.

Conclusion: Planning Your Puglia Adventure

Best Time to Visit Puglia

Puglia's Climate:

Puglia's Mediterranean climate is characterized by hot, dry summers and mild, wet winters. The region experiences a long tourist season, starting from late spring and lasting through early autumn. During this time, temperatures rise steadily, with an average high of around 30°C (86°F) in July and August, making it the hottest time of the year. Evenings and nights can still be pleasantly warm, making it a great time for outdoor dining and entertainment.

In contrast, winters in Puglia are mild, with average temperatures ranging from 8-15°C (46-59°F). While it is not particularly cold, the region can experience occasional cold spells, with temperatures dropping below freezing point in some areas. Rainfall is highest in November and December, but the region can experience scattered showers throughout the year, particularly in the fall and winter months.

Despite the cooler temperatures in the winter months, Puglia's climate is still suitable for outdoor activities, particularly during the spring and fall months. The region's natural beauty and mild weather make it ideal for exploring the countryside, hiking, and cycling.

Moreover, the region's long coastline, with its beautiful beaches, crystal-clear waters, and mild climate, is perfect for water sports such as swimming, snorkeling, and diving. The summer months are the best time for beach activities, with water temperatures ranging from 23-25°C (73-77°F) in July and August.

Additionally, Puglia's climate plays a significant role in the region's agriculture and culinary scene. The warm and dry weather during the summer months is ideal for growing many of the region's famous crops, including olives, grapes, and tomatoes. The fertile soil, combined with the region's abundant sunshine, contributes to the production of high-quality olive oil, wine, and other agricultural products.

Puglia is also famous for its cuisine, which is heavily influenced by its climate and agricultural practices. The region's long coastline offers an abundance of fresh seafood, while its fertile land produces an array of vegetables and fruits, which are used to create delicious and healthy dishes.

In the summer months, Puglia's cuisine focuses on light and refreshing dishes, such as salads, grilled seafood, and vegetables. The winter months, on the other hand, bring hearty dishes like soups, stews, and roasted meats.

Peak Season vs. Off-Season:

Peak season in Puglia from June to August is when the region sees the most visitors. This is due to the warm and sunny weather, making it a popular time to visit the beaches and coastal towns. However, with peak season comes higher accommodation prices, longer lines, and crowds at popular attractions. During these months, it is important to book accommodations and activities well in advance, as many places can be fully booked. While the summer months are a great time to visit Puglia's beaches, they may not be the ideal time to explore the region's other attractions, such as historic towns and cultural sites.

The shoulder seasons of spring (April to May) and fall (September to October) offer a pleasant climate with fewer crowds and lower prices. The mild temperatures make it a great time for outdoor activities, such as hiking and cycling. In spring, the countryside comes alive with wildflowers and greenery, while in the fall, the vineyards are full of ripe grapes waiting to be harvested. Many visitors find these seasons to be the best time to visit Puglia, as they offer a balance between good weather and fewer crowds.

The off-season, from November to March, can be a great time to explore Puglia's cultural and culinary offerings. The cooler temperatures make it a good time for city sightseeing, and the traditional festivals and events that take place during the winter months provide a unique insight into the local culture. However, it is important to note that some beach resorts and seasonal restaurants may be closed during this time. It is also worth noting that the weather can be unpredictable during the off-season, with occasional rain and chilly temperatures. Nonetheless, visitors who prefer to avoid the crowds and are willing to take the chance on the weather may find the off-season to be a rewarding time to visit Puglia.

Overall, the best time to visit Puglia depends on your personal preferences and what you want to experience during your trip. If you're looking for warm weather and the chance to soak up the sun on the beaches, then the peak season of June to August might be the best option for you. However, if you prefer milder weather, fewer crowds, and more affordable prices, then the shoulder seasons of spring and fall may be the best choice.

It's also worth considering that certain activities are more suited to specific times of the year. For example, if you're interested in wine tasting, then September and October are the ideal months to visit Puglia, as this is when the grape harvest takes place. On the other hand, if you want to experience the traditional olive harvesting and oil production methods, then November is the perfect time to visit.

Recommended Months for Specific Activities:

Beaches:
Puglia is known for its beautiful beaches with crystal-clear waters and stunning coastal scenery. The best time to visit the beaches is from June to September, when the weather is hot and sunny. During this time, most of the beach resorts and lidos are open, offering sun loungers, umbrellas, and beachside cafes. Some of the most popular beaches in Puglia include Torre dell'Orso, Pescoluse, and Porto Cesareo. It's worth noting that the beaches can get crowded during peak season, so it's best to arrive early to secure a good spot.

Hiking and Cycling:
Puglia's rolling hills, rugged coastline, and charming countryside make it a great destination for hiking and cycling. Spring (April to May) and fall (September to October) are the best times to explore the region on foot or by bike, when the weather is mild and the countryside is in bloom. Some of the most popular hiking and cycling trails include the Gargano Promontory, which offers stunning coastal views, and the Valle d'Itria, which takes you through picturesque villages and rolling hills. There are also several bike rental companies and guided tours available throughout the region.

Wine Tasting:
Puglia is home to some of Italy's most famous wines, such as Primitivo and Negroamaro. The grape harvest takes place in September and October, making these months a great time

to visit Puglia's wineries and taste some of the region's finest wines. Many wineries offer tours and tastings, allowing visitors to learn about the winemaking process and sample a variety of wines. Some of the best wineries to visit include Cantine Due Palme in Cellino San Marco, Tormaresca in Minervino Murge, and Leone de Castris in Salice Salentino.

Olive Harvesting:
Puglia is the largest olive oil producer in Italy, and November is the month when most of the region's olive groves are harvested. This is a great time to witness the traditional methods of olive picking and oil production, and to taste some of the freshest olive oil. Many local farms and agriturismi offer olive harvesting experiences, where visitors can pick olives and learn about the production process. Some of the best places to experience olive harvesting in Puglia include the town of Ostuni, known as the "White City" for its whitewashed buildings and olive groves, and the countryside around Bari.

Festivals and Events:
Puglia is a region rich in history and culture, and hosts many festivals and events throughout the year. Some of the most popular events include the Carnevale di Putignano in February, one of Italy's oldest and most famous carnivals; the Festival della Valle d'Itria in July and August, which showcases classical music and opera performances in the region's stunning baroque towns; and the Festa di San Nicola in December, a celebration of the patron saint of Bari. Checking the calendar of events is a great way to plan your trip and experience some of the region's unique cultural offerings.

Getting to and Around Puglia

Airports in Puglia:

Bari Karol Wojtyla Airport and Brindisi Airport are the two largest and busiest airports in Puglia. Bari Airport, located about 8 km from the city center, is the main airport in the region and handles both domestic and international flights. Brindisi Airport, located about 6 km from the city center, is the second busiest airport in Puglia and is also a hub for domestic and international flights. Both airports have modern facilities and amenities such as restaurants, cafes, shops, and car rental desks.

Foggia Gino Lisa Airport and Taranto-Grottaglie Airport are smaller airports that mainly serve domestic flights and regional routes. Foggia Airport is located in the northern part of Puglia and is a gateway to the Gargano Peninsula and the surrounding areas. Taranto-Grottaglie Airport is located in the southern part of Puglia and is a hub for business and private flights.

All four airports are well-connected to the region's main towns and cities via public transport such as trains, buses, and taxis. The easiest way to get from the airports to the city centers is by taxi or private transfer, which can be arranged in advance or upon arrival. There are also frequent shuttle buses that connect the airports to the city centers and main transport hubs such as train stations and bus terminals. Train services are also available from Bari and Brindisi airports, with direct connections to major cities such as Lecce, Taranto, and Matera. Buses are another convenient and affordable option, with services operated by companies such as Flixbus, Marino, and Pugliairbus.

Trains and Buses in Puglia:

Puglia's comprehensive rail and bus network is a convenient and affordable way to travel around the region. The regional train service, Ferrovie del Sud Est (FSE), is the main train operator in Puglia, providing frequent connections between major cities such as Bari, Brindisi, Lecce, and Taranto, as well as smaller towns and villages. The FSE trains are modern, comfortable, and air-conditioned, making them a great option for long journeys. The fares are also reasonable, with discounts available for students, seniors, and groups.

In addition to the FSE trains, there are also frequent bus services operated by the Società Trasporti Pubblici (STP) that connect smaller towns and villages that are not served by trains. The STP buses are modern, air-conditioned, and equipped with free Wi-Fi, making them a comfortable way to travel around the region. The fares are also affordable, with discounts available for frequent users and children.

Both train and bus tickets can be purchased at stations, online, or via mobile apps. Online ticketing is available through the FSE and STP websites, as well as through third-party ticketing platforms such as Trenitalia and GoEuro. Mobile apps such as FSE App and STP App allow travelers to purchase and store tickets on their smartphones, making it easy to access tickets on the go.

It's important to note that schedules and fares may vary depending on the season and demand, so it's always a good idea to check the latest information before traveling. Also, while the rail and bus network is extensive, some remote areas may not be well-served, so it's always a good idea to plan your itinerary in advance and make sure that transportation is available to your desired destinations.

Driving in Puglia:

Renting a car in Puglia can be a convenient way to travel around the region, especially if you want to explore off-the-beaten-path destinations that are not easily accessible by public transportation. With a rental car, you have the flexibility to set your own itinerary, stop wherever you like, and enjoy the scenic countryside at your own pace.

However, driving in Puglia can be a challenge, particularly for visitors who are not accustomed to narrow roads, aggressive drivers, and limited parking. The roads in Puglia are generally well-maintained, but some of them can be quite narrow, especially in the historic centers of the towns and villages. It is important to be aware of other drivers, as well as pedestrians and cyclists, who may be sharing the road with you.

Another challenge when driving in Puglia is the lack of signposting in some areas. While the major highways and tourist routes are usually well-signposted, some of the smaller country roads may not have clear markers or signs, making it difficult to navigate. In addition, GPS devices may not always be reliable in rural areas, so it's a good idea to have a backup plan, such as a paper map or directions from locals.

It's also important to note that some towns and cities in Puglia have limited traffic zones, known as ZTLs (Zona Traffico Limitato), where only authorized vehicles are allowed to enter. These zones are usually marked with signs and cameras, and entering them without permission can result in fines. If you are planning to drive in Puglia, it's a good idea to check if your destination has a ZTL, and if so, to park outside the zone and walk or take public transportation to your destination.

Finally, before renting a car in Puglia, it's important to check your car rental agreement for any hidden fees or insurance requirements. Some rental companies may require an international driver's license, and additional fees may apply for drivers under a certain age or for additional drivers. It's also a good idea to inspect the car carefully before driving off the rental lot, and to take note of any existing damage or scratches to avoid being charged for them later.

Bicycle Rentals and Tours:

Cycling is a great way to explore Puglia and experience its beautiful countryside and coastline up close. The region has a growing network of cycle paths and quiet country roads that offer scenic routes through olive groves, vineyards, and picturesque towns. Cycling in Puglia is suitable for all ages and skill levels, with routes ranging from easy coastal rides to more challenging mountain routes.

There are several bicycle rental shops in the main towns and cities of Puglia, such as Bari, Brindisi, Lecce, and Martina Franca. These shops offer a range of bikes, from standard road bikes to e-bikes and mountain bikes, as well as accessories like helmets, locks, and panniers. Some rental shops also offer guided tours that cater to different skill levels and interests, such as wine tasting tours, food tours, and cultural tours.

One of the most popular cycling routes in Puglia is the Ciclovia dell'Acquedotto Pugliese, a 260-km route that follows an aqueduct built in the early 20th century to transport water from the mountains to the towns and cities of Puglia. The route starts in Martina Franca and passes through picturesque towns such as Alberobello, Locorotondo, and Ostuni before ending in Brindisi. Along the way, cyclists can enjoy stunning views of the Valle d'Itria and the Adriatic Sea, as well as historic landmarks such as the trulli houses and the Romanesque cathedrals.

Another popular cycling route is the Coastal Cycling Route, a 200-km route that runs along the Adriatic coast from Otranto to Gargano National Park. The route passes through charming fishing villages, sandy beaches, and rocky cliffs, offering cyclists a chance to explore some of the region's most beautiful coastal landscapes. Highlights of the route include the historic town of Otranto, the natural reserve of Torre Guaceto, and the fishing village of Peschici.

The Valle d'Itria Cycling Route is another popular cycling route in Puglia, offering cyclists a chance to explore the picturesque Valle d'Itria, which is famous for its white-washed trulli houses and olive groves. The 200-km route starts in Martina Franca and passes through towns such as Cisternino, Ostuni, and Fasano before ending in Monopoli. Along the way, cyclists can enjoy the scenic countryside, visit local olive oil mills and wineries, and taste the delicious local cuisine.

If you plan to cycle in Puglia, it's important to wear a helmet, carry a map or GPS device, and check the weather forecast. It's also a good idea to bring plenty of water, snacks, and sunscreen, as some of the routes can be quite long and challenging. With its beautiful landscapes, rich history, and delicious cuisine, Puglia is a wonderful destination for cyclists of all levels.

Where to Stay in Puglia

Types of Accommodation:

Hotels and Resorts: Puglia has a wide range of hotels and resorts, from luxury five-star properties to more affordable options. Many hotels are located in historic buildings, such as palaces and convents, and offer amenities such as pools, spas, and restaurants. Some popular areas for hotels include the cities of Bari, Lecce, and Ostuni, as well as the coastal towns of Polignano a Mare, Monopoli, and Gallipoli.

Agriturismi: Agriturismi are farm stays that offer guests the chance to experience rural life in Puglia. These accommodations are often located on working farms and vineyards, and may offer activities such as cooking classes, wine tastings, and horseback riding. Agriturismi range from basic to luxurious, and can be a great way to connect with nature and the local culture.

Trulli and Masserie: Trulli are traditional conical stone houses that are unique to Puglia, particularly in the Valle d'Itria region. Many trulli have been converted into vacation rentals or bed and breakfasts, offering guests the chance to stay in a charming and historic setting. Masserie are fortified farmhouses that are also common in Puglia, especially in the Salento area. Many masserie have been restored and converted into boutique hotels or vacation rentals, often featuring pools, gardens, and restaurants.

Apartments and Villas: For longer stays or larger groups, renting an apartment or villa can be a good option. Puglia has many vacation rental options, ranging from small apartments in historic buildings to large villas with pools and gardens. Some popular rental websites for Puglia include Airbnb, HomeAway, and VRBO.

Recommended Areas to Stay in Puglia:

Bari: Bari is the largest city in Puglia and a major transportation hub, making it a convenient base for exploring the region. The old town (Bari Vecchia) is full of historic buildings, narrow alleys, and lively piazzas, and offers a range of accommodations from budget hostels to luxury hotels. The seaside neighborhood of Bari Palese is also a popular area for hotels and resorts.

Lecce: Known as the "Florence of the South," Lecce is a charming baroque city with beautiful churches, palaces, and piazzas. The historic center (Centro Storico) is full of narrow streets and hidden courtyards, and offers a range of accommodations from boutique hotels to guesthouses. The nearby countryside is also dotted with agriturismi and masserie.

Ostuni: Known as the "White City," Ostuni is a picturesque hilltop town with whitewashed houses and stunning views of the surrounding countryside. The old town (Città Vecchia) is a maze of narrow alleys and staircases, and offers a range of accommodations from B&Bs to luxury hotels. The nearby coast is also a popular area for vacation rentals and resorts.

Salento: The Salento peninsula is the southernmost part of Puglia and is known for its stunning beaches, crystal-clear waters, and vibrant towns. The towns of Otranto, Gallipoli, and Santa Maria di Leuca are popular areas for accommodations, ranging from B&Bs to luxury hotels. The countryside is also full of agriturismi and masserie, offering a peaceful retreat from the coast.

Unique Accommodation Options:

Glamping: For a unique and eco-friendly experience, consider glamping (glamorous camping) in Puglia. There are a variety of glamping options available, ranging from tents and yurts to eco-pods and treehouses. Many glamping sites offer amenities such as hot tubs, fire pits, and outdoor kitchens, and can be a great way to connect with nature while still enjoying some luxury.

Cave Hotels: Puglia is home to many caves, and some of these have been converted into unique hotels and accommodations. Staying in a cave hotel can be a truly unforgettable experience, offering a cool and tranquil escape from the summer heat. Some popular cave hotels in Puglia include Le Grotte della Civita in Matera and La Dimora delle Grotte in Castellana Grotte.

Monasteries and Convents: Puglia has a rich history of monasteries and convents, many of which have been converted into unique accommodations. Staying in a monastery or convent can be a peaceful and contemplative experience, and many of these buildings have been beautifully restored and offer modern amenities. Some popular options include the Convento di Santa Maria degli Angeli in Conversano and the Monastero Santa Maria di Costantinopoli in Gallipoli.

Overall, Puglia offers a wide range of accommodations to suit every budget and taste. Whether you're looking for a luxury resort or a rustic farm stay, there's something for everyone in this beautiful and diverse region. When planning your trip, consider the type of experience you want to have and choose your accommodation accordingly.

Tips for Traveling in Puglia.

Language:
When traveling to Puglia, it's always a good idea to learn some basic Italian phrases to help you navigate and communicate with locals. While English is spoken in most tourist areas, outside of these areas, you may find that locals speak only Italian or regional dialects. Therefore, it's important to have a basic understanding of the language to help you communicate effectively.

Some basic Italian phrases to learn include greetings, such as "ciao" (hello/goodbye), "buongiorno" (good morning), and "buonasera" (good evening). You may also want to learn how to ask for directions or help, such as "Dove si trova...?" (Where is...?) or "Posso avere un po' di aiuto?" (Can I have some help?). Additionally, knowing some common phrases for ordering food and drinks, such as "un caffè" (a coffee) or "una birra" (a beer), can come in handy when dining out.

While it's not necessary to become fluent in Italian before your trip, taking the time to learn some basic phrases can go a long way in helping you navigate the region and communicate effectively with locals. You can find language learning resources online, such as language apps or online courses, or consider taking a class at a local language school. Additionally, many guidebooks and travel websites offer helpful language guides and phrasebooks specifically for travelers.

Currency and Payment:
When traveling to Puglia, it's important to be aware of the currency and payment options available to you. The Euro (EUR) is the official currency in Italy, and it's the only currency accepted in Puglia. You can exchange your currency at the airport or at banks, but keep in mind that exchange rates may vary depending on the location and the time of day.

Credit cards are widely accepted in Puglia, especially in larger cities and tourist areas. Most major credit cards such as Visa, Mastercard, and American Express are accepted in Puglia, but it's always a good idea to check with your bank or credit card company before you travel to make sure your card will work in Italy.

However, it's still a good idea to have some cash on hand, especially in smaller towns and rural areas where credit card acceptance may be limited. ATMs are widely available throughout Puglia, and you can withdraw cash using your debit or credit card. Be aware that some ATMs may charge a fee for using foreign cards, so check with your bank before you travel to avoid any surprises.

When using credit cards or withdrawing cash from ATMs, be aware of exchange rates and any fees that may apply. Some banks and credit card companies charge a foreign transaction fee for purchases made outside your home country, so it's important to factor in these additional costs when planning your budget for your trip.

In summary, while credit cards are widely accepted in Puglia, it's always a good idea to have some cash on hand, especially in smaller towns and rural areas. ATMs are widely available, but be aware of any fees and exchange rates when using them. It's also important to check with your bank or credit card company before you travel to ensure that your card will work in Italy and to avoid any unexpected fees or charges.

Safety and Security:
Puglia is a safe region for travelers, but it's always important to take basic safety precautions to ensure a hassle-free and enjoyable trip. Here are some tips to keep in mind:

Keep an eye on your personal belongings: Pickpocketing can be a problem in crowded areas such as train stations, markets, and tourist sites. Be aware of your surroundings and keep your valuables close to you. Use a money belt or a secure bag to carry your passport, cash, and credit cards.

Avoid deserted areas at night: While Puglia is generally safe, it's always a good idea to avoid walking alone at night in deserted areas, especially if you are not familiar with the area. Stick to well-lit streets and busy areas, and if you do need to travel at night, consider taking a taxi or using public transportation.

Use common sense: When it comes to personal safety, it's always best to use common sense. Avoid getting too intoxicated, especially if you are traveling alone. Be aware of your surroundings and trust your instincts. If something seems suspicious or too good to be true, it probably is.

Be aware of scammers: While Puglia is generally safe, there are always scammers looking to take advantage of unsuspecting tourists. Be aware of common scams such as people offering to help you with your bags, fake petitions, or fake charity collectors. If someone is asking for money or trying to sell you something, be cautious and use your judgment.

Know the emergency numbers: It's always a good idea to know the local emergency numbers, such as the police, ambulance, and fire department. Keep these numbers handy in case of an emergency.

By following these basic safety precautions, you can ensure a safe and enjoyable trip to Puglia. Remember to always be aware of your surroundings, trust your instincts, and use common sense.

Etiquette and Customs:
Dress Code: Puglia is a region with many religious sites, and it's important to dress modestly when visiting these sites out of respect for local customs. This means avoiding shorts, short skirts, tank tops, and other revealing clothing. It's also a good idea to bring a scarf or shawl to cover your head and

shoulders when entering churches and other religious buildings.

Greetings: In Puglia, it's customary to greet others with a handshake and a kiss on each cheek (starting with the left). This is true not only in formal settings, but also when meeting new people in casual social situations. When addressing someone who is older or in a position of authority, use their formal title (e.g. "Signore" or "Signora").

Table Manners: Italians take food very seriously, and there are certain customs and etiquette rules to keep in mind when dining in Puglia. For example, it's considered impolite to start eating before everyone at the table has been served. It's also common to use a fork and knife for most dishes, including pizza, and to avoid using your hands to eat bread or other foods.

Tipping: Tipping is not always expected in Puglia, but it's appreciated for exceptional service. In restaurants, it's customary to round up the bill or leave a small amount (around 10% of the total) as a tip. It's also common to tip taxi drivers, hairdressers, and other service providers, although the amount is usually small (e.g. rounding up to the nearest Euro).

It's important to remember that Puglia is a region with strong cultural traditions, and showing respect for these traditions is an important part of being a polite and respectful visitor. By keeping these customs and etiquette tips in mind, you'll be better equipped to navigate social situations and make a positive impression on locals.

Additional Resources:
Guidebooks: Guidebooks are a great resource for planning your trip to Puglia. They provide detailed information on

local attractions, restaurants, accommodations, and transportation. Popular guidebooks for Puglia include Lonely Planet, Rick Steves, and Fodor's.

Online forums: Online forums are a great way to connect with other travelers and get insider tips and advice. TripAdvisor is one of the most popular travel forums, with a wealth of information on Puglia and other destinations around the world. Other forums to consider include Lonely Planet's Thorn Tree Forum and Fodor's Travel Talk.

Travel blogs: Travel blogs offer a personal perspective on traveling in Puglia, with detailed accounts of experiences and recommendations. Some popular Puglia travel blogs include Puglia Guide, Puglia Positiva, and Puglia on my Mind.

Official tourism website: The official tourism website of Puglia (www.viaggiareinpuglia.it) is a great resource for planning your trip. It offers information on local attractions, events, accommodations, and transportation. You can also find contact information for local tourism offices and book guided tours and activities through the website.

Travel agents and tour operators: If you prefer to have someone else handle the details of your trip, you can consult with a travel agent or tour operator. They can help you plan your itinerary, book your accommodations and transportation, and arrange guided tours and activities. Some popular tour operators in Puglia include ItalyXP, Puglia Private Tour, and The Thinking Traveller.

Made in United States
Troutdale, OR
05/09/2024

19763236R00050